transformation

EMBRACING SPIRITUAL GROWTH

SKINNY BROWN DOG
MEDIA
EST. 2013
ATLANTA | PUNTA DEL ESTE

For Information, Contact:
Distributed by Skinny Brown Dog Media
SkinnyBrownDogMedia.com
Email: Info@SkinnyBrownDogMedia.com

Transformation
Embracing Spiritual Growth
By Eric G Reid
Part of the Whole Life Devotional Series

Library of Congress Catalog in Publication Data
ISBN eBook   978-1-965235-29-4
ISBN trade paperback   978-1-965235-26-3
ISBN Hardback Dust Jacketed   978-1-965235-28-7
ISBN case laminate   978-1-965235-27-0

CONTENTS

WEEK 3
EMBRACING YOUR ROLE AS A
LEADER AND LIGHT

DEDICATION

To my son, Ignacio,

You have transformed me and the world around you.
May your spiritual journey be filled with growth, strength, and unwavering faith. You inspire me to be a better person, and I am grateful for the incredible impact you have on my life.

Thank you for walking this journey with me.

"As iron sharpens iron, so one person sharpens another."
—Proverbs 27:17

Transformation

Welcome to "Transformation: Embracing Spiritual Growth." Picture this journey as a grand road trip with a close friend—me! We've got our map (the Bible), GPS (the Holy Spirit), and plenty of snacks (spiritual wisdom) for the ride. Think of it like the first time I tried baking homemade bread—full of excitement, a bit of uncertainty, and a few "What on earth am I doing?" moments. But don't worry, we'll navigate the twists and turns together, and maybe even have some fun along the way.

This devotional is your trusty travel guide, packed with insights, reflections, and practical steps to help you grow spiritually. Just like a good road trip is about more than the destination, our focus here is on the journey of transformation. It's about those small daily choices that lead to significant change over time. It's about letting God work in the ordinary moments of life, transforming us little by little.

Ever hear people say that becoming a new creature in Christ is like getting an upgrade you didn't even know you needed? It's like discovering a hidden feature on your smartphone—you've been using it for calls and texts, and suddenly you realize it can do so much more! That's the kind of transformation we're talking about here. It's not just about adding new features but unlocking the full potential of who God created you to be.

Navigating spiritual growth in our modern world can feel like a rollercoaster. We're surrounded by a cacophony of voices—media, society, even our friends and family—each with their own take on what it means to be spiritually mature. These competing messages can leave us feeling lost, confused, and spiritually parched as we try to discern what true transformation looks like and how to achieve it.

I remember when I first started my journey of faith. I thought spiritual growth was a checklist: read the Bible, pray, go to church. But I quickly realized it's so much more than that. It's about transformation—about letting God's Word penetrate your heart and change your life. It's about becoming more like Christ every day. And yes, it's a journey with its bumps and detours, but it's also filled with incredible discoveries and profound growth.

So, buckle up, keep your sense of humor handy, and let's set out on this exciting journey of transformation together. With God as our guide, we're in for a ride filled with growth, discovery, and perhaps a few surprises. Welcome to the adventure!

Why This Study?

Ever wonder why people say becoming a new creature in Christ is like getting an upgrade you didn't even know you needed? It's like discovering a hidden feature on your smartphone—you've been using it for calls and texts, and suddenly you realize it can do so much more! That's the kind of transformation we're talking about here. It's not just about adding new features but unlocking the full potential of who God created you to be.

Navigating spiritual growth in our modern world can feel like a rollercoaster. We are surrounded by a cacophony of voices—media, society, even our friends and family—each with their own take on what it means to be spiritually mature. These competing messages can leave us feeling lost, confused, and spiritually parched as we try to discern what true transformation looks like and how to achieve it.

When I first started my journey of faith, I thought spiritual growth was a checklist of things to do: read the Bible, pray, go to church. But I quickly realized it's so much more than that. It's about transformation—letting God's Word penetrate your heart and change your life. It's about becoming more like Christ every day. And yes, it's a journey with bumps and detours, but it's also filled with incredible discoveries and profound growth.

This study is designed to help you cut through the noise and focus on what truly matters: your relationship with God. By dedicating time each day to study the Bible, pray, and reflect, you will cultivate a deeper and more resilient faith. This devotional is not just about gaining knowledge; it is about transformation. It's about allowing God's Word to penetrate your heart and change your life.

As we embark on this journey together, let's keep an open heart and mind, ready for the changes God wants to make in us. Remember, it's not about perfection but progress. Each step we take brings us closer to understanding and embracing the full, abundant life God has for us.

The Importance of Spiritual Growth

Spiritual growth isn't just a "nice to have" aspect of our Christian life; it's essential. Think of it like a plant that needs water, sunlight, and good soil to thrive. Without these elements, the plant will wither and die. Similarly, our spiritual lives need nurturing through prayer, Bible study, and other spiritual disciplines to grow and flourish.

When we embrace spiritual growth, we allow God to transform us from the inside out. This transformation helps us align our lives more closely with His will, making us more effective in our faith and witness. It's not just about gaining knowledge but about letting that knowledge change us. As we grow spiritually, we develop a deeper relationship with God, which brings us closer to understanding His purpose for our lives.

But why is spiritual growth so important? Let me share a personal experience. When I first started my faith journey, I was content with a surface-level understanding. I thought attending church and reading the Bible occasionally would be enough. However, I soon realized that my faith felt shallow and unfulfilling. It wasn't until I committed to growing spiritually that I began to experience real change. I started to see God working in my life in ways I never imagined. I felt more peace, joy, and purpose than ever before.

Spiritual growth also equips us to handle life's challenges better. When we are grounded in our faith, we can face difficulties with a sense of hope and resilience. The Bible tells us in James 1:2-4, "Consider it pure joy, my brothers and sisters, whenever you face trials of many kinds, because you know that the testing of your faith produces perseverance. Let perseverance finish its work so that you may be mature and complete, not lacking anything." This passage highlights that trials are a part of our spiritual growth journey. They refine us and help us become mature in our faith.

Moreover, spiritual growth fosters community and connection with other believers. As we grow, we naturally want to share our experiences and support others in their journey. This creates a strong, vibrant faith community where we can encourage and uplift each other. We become more empathetic, understanding, and supportive, reflecting Christ's love in our interactions.

Growing spiritually also impacts how we serve others. When we are spiritually mature, we are more attuned to the needs around us and more willing to step out in faith to meet those needs. Our actions become a reflection of our faith, drawing others to Christ through our example. As Jesus said in Matthew 5:16, "Let your light shine before others, that they may see your good deeds and glorify your Father in heaven."

Finally, spiritual growth leads to a deeper understanding and application of God's Word. The Bible becomes more than just a book; it becomes a living, breathing guide that shapes our thoughts, actions, and decisions. We start to see its relevance in every aspect of our lives and are better equipped to live out its teachings.

In summary, spiritual growth is crucial because it transforms us, equips us to handle challenges, fosters community, enhances our service to others, and deepens our understanding of God's Word. It's a lifelong journey that brings us closer to God and helps us live out our faith more fully. As we embark on this study, let's commit to growing spiritually and allowing God to work in and through us.

What Can Be Gained?

Engaging with this study offers numerous benefits:

- Clarity and Confidence: By understanding your spiritual growth in Christ, you will gain clarity about your purpose and direction in life. This newfound clarity will empower you to make decisions confidently and live with a sense of intentionality and purpose.
- Spiritual Growth: Daily engagement with scripture and reflective questions will deepen your relationship with God. As you spend time in prayer and meditation, you will become more attuned to His voice and guidance.

- Resilience Against Worldly Pressures: By recognizing and resisting the influences of worldly spiritual standards, you will develop resilience. This will help you stand firm in your faith even when faced with challenges and temptations.

- Authentic Community: Understanding the importance of community and support in your spiritual journey will encourage you to build and maintain meaningful relationships with fellow believers. These connections will provide encouragement, accountability, and a sense of belonging.

- Practical Application: Each day's action plan provides practical steps to apply what you've learned, making the principles of godly spiritual growth a tangible part of your daily life. This will help you integrate your faith into every aspect of your existence.

- Inner Peace and Joy: Discovering and living out your true spiritual growth in God brings a profound sense of peace and joy. You will experience the contentment that comes from knowing you are loved and valued by your Creator and that your life has a meaningful purpose.

Journey of Transformation

This study is not just about gaining knowledge; it is about transformation. As you work through each day's readings and reflections, allow the Holy Spirit to work in your heart and mind. Be open to the changes that God wants to make in your life. Embrace the process of becoming who He has created you to be.

Transformation requires intentionality. It involves making a conscious effort to align your thoughts, attitudes, and actions with

God's truth. This study will guide you through this process, providing the tools and support you need to grow and mature in your faith.

I remember a time when I felt stuck in my spiritual journey. It seemed like no matter what I did, I wasn't moving forward. Then I realized that transformation is a daily choice, not a onetime event. It's about small, consistent steps that lead to significant change over time. It's about letting God work in the ordinary moments of life, transforming us little by little.

As we go through this study, we will encounter various aspects of spiritual growth—from renewing our minds to deepening our relationship with God. Each day's reading and reflection is designed to challenge and encourage you to embrace the transformative work of the Holy Spirit.

How to Use This Devotional

Each day of this devotional is structured to provide a holistic approach to understanding and embracing your spiritual growth. Here's how to make the most of it:

1. Scripture Readings: Begin each day by reading the suggested scriptures. Take your time to read and reflect on the passages, allowing God's Word to speak to your heart.
2. Devotional Thought: Read the devotional thought for the day. These reflections are designed to help you understand and apply the scriptures to your life. Spend time journaling about what you've read and how it resonates with you.
3. Questions for Reflection: Spend time pondering the reflection questions. These questions are meant to provoke deep thought and

personal application. Consider journaling your responses to capture your insights and growth.

4. Daily Action Plan: Each day includes a practical action step to help you live out the principles you've learned. These actions will reinforce your understanding and encourage you to integrate godly spiritual growth into your daily life.

5. Prayer: End each day with a time of prayer. Ask God to help you embrace your spiritual growth and to guide you in living out His purpose for your life.

Remember, this journey is for you. If a day takes a week to work through, that's okay. The gift of this time is about reading, reflection, and prayer designed uniquely for you. Relax and let the process unfold in God's timing.

Welcome to a journey of deepening faith and transformation. Whether you're at the beginning of your spiritual journey or looking to reignite your passion for growth, this study is designed to help you understand and embrace the ongoing process of becoming more Christlike. May God bless you richly as you seek to grow in His grace and knowledge.

PREPARING FOR THE JOURNEY AHEAD

As we prepare to dive into this three-week journey, let's set our hearts and minds on the path ahead. Think of this as the first leg of our road trip. We're fueling up the car, checking the map, and maybe even packing some of our favorite snacks. It's a time of anticipation and preparation. Just like any journey, we need to be ready for the adventure ahead, and that starts with setting our intentions and aligning our hearts with God's purpose.

Spiritual growth is a bit like tending a garden. It requires patience, effort, and the right conditions. We'll be planting seeds of faith, watering them with prayer and scripture, and weeding out anything that hinders our growth. It's a process that takes time and dedication, but the harvest is well worth it.

This week, we'll focus on understanding what true transformation looks like. We'll dig into the Word, seeking insights and guidance on how to renew our minds and embrace the changes God wants to bring about in our lives. We'll also learn to navigate the obstacles that inevitably arise, trusting that God is with us every step of the way.

Let's commit to this journey of growth and transformation, trusting that God will guide us every step of the way. Take a moment to pray, asking God to open your heart and mind to His truth and to prepare you for the changes He wants to make in your life. Remember, we're in this together, and with God as our guide, we can't go wrong.

Welcome to a journey of deepening faith and transformation. May God bless you richly as you seek to grow in His grace and knowledge. Now, let's roll up our sleeves, prepare for the unexpected, and embark on this incredible journey of becoming more like Christ.

WEEK 1
Understanding Transformation

Welcome to Week 1 of our journey into embracing spiritual growth through transformation. Think of this week as setting out on a road trip with a good friend. We have our map (the Bible), our guide (the Holy Spirit), and a sense of adventure as we explore new spiritual landscapes. Transformation, in this context, is like upgrading our old, rusty vehicle to a sleek, new model—one that runs smoother, is more reliable, and can take us further than we ever imagined.

Transformation is not a onetime event but an ongoing process that requires our willingness to be molded and shaped by God's hands. It involves a deliberate choice to turn away from old patterns and embrace new ways of thinking and living that reflect God's will for our lives. This week, we will delve into the process of spiritual transformation, the renewal of our minds, and the importance of embracing change.

We will also look at the common obstacles that hinder our transformation and how we can overcome them with God's help. By understanding these key principles, we can begin to see how God works in our lives to shape us into His image.

Transformation is a journey that involves continuous growth and development. It's about allowing God's grace to work through us, making us more compassionate, patient, and loving. As we go through this week, let's commit to being open and receptive to the changes God wants to bring about in our lives. Let's trust in His perfect plan and embrace the process with faith and courage.

Key Themes

- The Process of Transformation
- Renewing Your Mind

- Embracing Change
- Overcoming Obstacles
- Trusting God's Plan

Anchor Scripture

"Do not conform to the pattern of this world but be transformed by the renewing of your mind. Then you will be able to test and approve what God's will is—his good, pleasing and perfect will."
—Romans 12:2

Reflection

As we begin this week, let's take some time to reflect on what transformation means in the context of our spiritual journey. Consider how the process of transformation has played out in your life so far. Have there been moments where you've experienced significant change, growth, or renewal? How did those moments shape your faith and relationship with God?

Think about the areas in your life where you feel the need for transformation. What aspects of your character, mindset, or behavior could benefit from God's transforming power? As we go through the daily readings and reflections this week, let's open our hearts to the work of the Holy Spirit, allowing Him to guide us and change us from the inside out.

Welcome to a journey of deepening faith and transformation. Whether you're at the beginning of your spiritual journey or looking to reignite your passion for growth, this week is designed to help you understand and embrace the ongoing process of becoming more Christlike. May God bless you richly as you seek to grow in His grace and knowledge.

DAY 1
THE PROCESS OF
TRANSFORMATION

Have you ever felt like you're stuck in the same place, unable to move forward in your spiritual journey? I remember a time when I felt stagnant in my faith, despite my efforts to grow. I was just turning pages and checking boxes, but nothing seemed to be making "big waves." It wasn't until I understood that transformation is a continuous process that I started seeing my faith as something to be achieved and instead something to be experienced.

I know it sounds silly, but I approached my faith journey much like one of those 75-Day Hard Body challenges. You know the ones—commit to a routine, dive all in, and at the end of 75 days, you emerge as a perfectly refined version of yourself. I thought if I just followed a strict regimen of prayer, Bible reading, and church attendance, I'd become a fully formed, perfectly refined man of faith. But here's the thing: faith doesn't work on a 75-day plan. It's a lifelong journey, full of ups and downs, twists and turns, and plenty of unexpected detours.

Our spiritual growth works in much the same way. It's not about achieving perfection overnight but about growing a little more each day. It's about the process, the journey, and the small, incremental changes that add up over time. When I shifted my mindset from trying to achieve something to experiencing and embracing the journey, my faith began to flourish.

Instead of getting frustrated with myself for not being "perfect," I started to appreciate the process. I found joy in the small steps, the everyday moments where God was working in my life. I learned to trust that even when I couldn't see it, God was shaping and refining me.

So, if you're feeling stuck or stagnant in your spiritual journey, remember that transformation is a continuous process. It's not about racing to the finish line but about walking with God each day, allowing Him to work in and through you. Embrace the journey, celebrate the small victories, and trust that God is at work, even when you can't see the progress.

Role Models in Scripture

In the story of Nicodemus, we see a journey of transformation that is both profound and inspiring. Nicodemus, a Pharisee and member of the Jewish ruling council, came to Jesus at night, seeking understanding. This encounter is significant because it shows Nicodemus' willingness to seek truth despite the potential backlash from his peers.

Imagine Nicodemus slipping through the dark streets, his heart pounding with a mix of fear and anticipation. As a respected teacher, he had everything to lose by associating with Jesus, yet something about Jesus' message stirred his soul. When he finally met Jesus, the conversation took an unexpected turn. Jesus spoke of being "born again" to see the kingdom of God (John 3:1-21). This concept of spiritual rebirth was revolutionary for Nicodemus. He was a learned man, well-versed in the Scriptures, yet he struggled to grasp this new teaching. Jesus patiently explained the necessity of being born of water and the Spirit, emphasizing that flesh gives birth to flesh, but the Spirit gives birth to spirit.

Nicodemus' transformation was not immediate. He didn't leave that night as a fully convinced disciple but rather with a seed planted in his heart. We see him again in John 7:50-52, where he cautiously defends Jesus before the Sanhedrin, suggesting that they should hear Jesus out before condemning Him. This act, though small, indicates the beginning of his transformation. Nicodemus was starting to move from curiosity to cautious advocacy.

The final and most significant appearance of Nicodemus is in John 19:39-42, where he assists Joseph of Arimathea in preparing Jesus' body for burial. This act of devotion and bravery marks a significant transformation from a secret seeker to a bold disciple. Nicodemus brought a mixture of myrrh and aloes, about seventy-five pounds in weight, a considerable and costly amount. He openly associated with Jesus in His death, showing a deep respect and belief that had grown over time.

Nicodemus' journey teaches us that transformation is a process that involves seeking, learning, and growing in our faith. It's about moving from curiosity to commitment, from fear to faith. His story is a powerful reminder that transformation takes time and that every step we take towards Jesus is a step in the right direction. Just like Nicodemus, we might not have all the answers right away, but our willingness to seek, ask questions, and act on what we learn leads us towards spiritual growth and a deeper relationship with God.

Scripture to Remember

"Do not conform to the pattern of this world but be transformed by the renewing of your mind."
—Romans 12:2

"Therefore, if anyone is in Christ, the new creation has come: The old has gone, the new is here!"
—2 Corinthians 5:17

"And we all, who with unveiled faces contemplate the Lord's glory, are being transformed into his image with ever increasing glory, which comes from the Lord, who is the Spirit."
—2 Corinthians 3:18

Consider This

Transformation is a journey, not a destination. It's about continually growing closer to God and allowing His Spirit to change us from the inside out.

Questions for Reflection

1. What areas of your life need transformation?

_____

_____

_____

2. How can you embrace the process of transformation in your daily life?

_____

_____

_____

3. What steps can you take to seek truth and understanding, like Nicodemus?

_____

_____

_____

4. How can you move from curiosity to commitment in your faith journey?

_____

_____

_____

Living Out Our Transformation

Create a daily routine that includes time for prayer, scripture reading, and reflection. Focus on allowing God to transform your thoughts and actions.

_____

_____

_____

_____

_____

Building Deeper Connection to Transformation

- Journaling Prompt: Reflect on a time when you experienced a significant transformation. What triggered that change, and how did it affect your relationship with God?
- Suggested Prayer: "Lord, help me to embrace the process of transformation. Change me from the inside out and help me to grow closer to You each day. Amen."

Tomorrow's Journey

Tomorrow, we'll delve into renewing our minds and how it affects our spiritual growth. Embrace the journey of transformation, trusting in God's perfect plan.

DAY 2
RENEWING YOUR MIND

Have you ever found yourself trapped in a cycle of negative thoughts, feeling like they dictate your every move? I remember a particularly tough time when doubt and fear seemed to rule my mind. It was as if every decision I made was clouded by these oppressive thoughts, making it hard to see any light at the end of the tunnel.

I'd be lying if I said I've completely conquered those feelings. In fact, just this morning, I found myself battling a fresh wave of anxiety about a big project. But here's the thing—I've learned that peace and confidence aren't permanent states of being. They're more like destinations on a map that I know how to reach when the journey gets tough.

The turning point for me was discovering how to renew my mind with God's truth. It's like when you find a shortcut to a place you visit often. Once you know the way, it becomes easier to get there each time. By immersing myself in Scripture and prayer, I've found a way to navigate through the fog of negative thoughts to a place of clarity and reassurance.

Role Models in Scripture

In Romans 12:2, Paul encourages believers to renew their minds to be transformed. This renewal is about changing the way we think to align with God's truth. A profound example of this is the story of Saul's conversion to Paul (Acts 9:1-19). Saul was a zealous Pharisee who persecuted Christians, believing he was upholding the Jewish law. His mind was set on eradicating the followers of Jesus, whom he saw as a threat to Judaism. However, on the road to Damascus, Saul encountered the risen Christ in a blinding light. Jesus asked him, "Saul, Saul, why do you persecute me?" This question struck Saul to the core, initiating a profound transformation.

Blinded by the encounter, Saul was led into Damascus, where he spent three days in darkness, fasting and praying. During this time, God spoke to Ananias, instructing him to visit Saul. Ananias, though initially hesitant, obeyed and laid hands on Saul, restoring his sight and filling him with the Holy Spirit. This experience completely renewed Saul's mind. He went from being a persecutor of Christians to a fervent apostle of Christ, taking on the new name Paul. Paul's transformation illustrates the power of a renewed mind and how it can radically change our lives. He dedicated the rest of his life to spreading the gospel, writing many of the New Testament letters that continue to guide and inspire Christians today.

Paul's journey reminds us that no matter how entrenched we might be in our current ways of thinking, encountering God's truth can lead to radical transformation. His story shows that even those who seem farthest from God can be renewed and used powerfully for His purposes. This kind of change requires openness, humility, and a willingness to let go of old mindsets in favor of God's transformative truth.

Scripture to Remember

"Set your minds on things above, not on earthly things."
—Colossians 3:2

"Finally, brothers and sisters, whatever is true, whatever is noble, whatever is right, whatever is pure, whatever is lovely, whatever is admirable—if anything is excellent or praiseworthy—think about such things."
—Philippians 4:8

"The mind governed by the Spirit is life and peace."
—Romans 8:6

Consider This

Renewing our minds is a daily practice. It involves filling our thoughts with God's truth and letting go of negative patterns that hinder our spiritual growth.

Questions for Reflection

1. What negative thought patterns do you need to let go of?

_____

_____

_____

2. How can you start renewing your mind today?

_____

_____

_____

3. What steps can you take to align your thoughts with God's truth?

_____

_____

_____

4. How does Paul's transformation inspire you to change your own mindset?

_____

_____

_____

Living Out Our Transformation

Make a conscious effort to replace negative thoughts with God's truth. Memorize scriptures that speak to your struggles and meditate on them daily.

_____

_____

_____

_____

_____

_____

_____

_____

_____

_____

Building Deeper Connection to Transformation

- Journaling Prompt: Write about a negative thought pattern you struggle with and how you can replace it with a positive, God centered truth.
- Suggested Prayer: "Lord, renew my mind with Your truth. Help me to focus on things that are true, noble, and praiseworthy, and to let go of negative thoughts. Amen."

Tomorrow's Journey

Tomorrow, we'll explore embracing change and how it can lead to growth and blessings. Keep renewing your mind and watch how it transforms your life!

DAY 3
EMBRACING CHANGE

Change can be daunting, can't it? I remember when I had to move to a new city for the first time as a "grown-up." The uncertainty was overwhelming. There were days I thought I would just be defeated by all the things that were changing. The thought of leaving behind familiar surroundings, friends, and routines was intimidating. I questioned if I was making the right decision and worried about all the unknowns that lay ahead.

But something amazing happened when I started to embrace that change. I began to see it as an adventure rather than a burden. I was led to new opportunities and growth I never imagined. I met incredible people who enriched my life, discovered new passions, and experienced personal growth in ways I hadn't anticipated. Now, I look back on that time with gratitude. It taught me resilience, adaptability, and the importance of stepping out of my comfort zone. Now I love a good move—it's the packing and unpacking I hate.

Embracing change can be challenging, but it also opens the door to new beginnings and unexpected blessings. It reminds us that with faith and a positive mindset, we can navigate through the uncertainties of life and emerge stronger and more fulfilled.

Role Models in Scripture

The story of Ruth beautifully illustrates the power of embracing change. Ruth, a Moabite woman, faced significant changes when her husband died. Instead of returning to her people and their gods, she chose to stay with her mother-in-law, Naomi, and embrace Naomi's God and people (Ruth 1:16-17). This decision marked the beginning of a remarkable journey of faith and transformation. Ruth's choice to embrace change led her to Bethlehem, where she gleaned in the fields to provide for Naomi and herself.

Her dedication and hard work caught the attention of Boaz, a wealthy relative of Naomi. Boaz showed kindness and protection to Ruth, allowing her to gather grain in his fields. Ruth's loyalty and willingness to embrace change led to a series of events that would drastically alter her life. Naomi guided Ruth to seek Boaz as a kinsman-redeemer, a practice in Israelite culture where a close relative could marry a widow to preserve the family lineage. Ruth followed Naomi's advice, and Boaz, impressed by Ruth's character and kindness, agreed to marry her. Their union not only provided security for Ruth and Naomi but also positioned Ruth in the lineage of King David and, ultimately, Jesus Christ.

Ruth's story demonstrates that embracing change, even when it's challenging, can lead to unexpected blessings and fulfillment of God's greater plan. Her faith, loyalty, and courage inspire us to trust God during times of change, knowing that He is at work in every season of our lives. This story serves as a powerful reminder that change, while often difficult and uncertain, can open the door to new opportunities and divine intervention.

Ruth's journey was not an easy one. She left behind her homeland, family, and everything familiar to follow Naomi into a new culture and faith. It was a leap of faith driven by love and loyalty, but it was also fraught with challenges. Ruth had to navigate the uncertainties of a new land, find a way to provide for herself and Naomi, and adapt to a culture that was not her own. Despite these challenges, Ruth's unwavering commitment to Naomi and her faith in God propelled her forward.

As Ruth worked in the fields, she demonstrated perseverance and humility. Her actions caught the attention of Boaz, not just because of her hard work, but because of her character. Boaz recognized Ruth's kindness and dedication, and his response was one of protection and provision. This interaction between Ruth and Boaz shows how God's providence works through our actions and relationships. When we embrace change with faith and integrity, God often brings people into our lives who can help and support us.

The culmination of Ruth's story is truly inspiring. Her marriage to Boaz and the birth of their son Obed secured her place in the lineage of King David and Jesus Christ. This outcome was far beyond what Ruth could have imagined when she first decided to stay with Naomi. It shows that when we trust God and embrace the changes He brings into our lives, we open ourselves up to His extraordinary plans. Ruth's story encourages us to face change with courage and faith, knowing that God's hand is guiding us towards His perfect will.

Scripture to Remember

"For I know the plans I have for you, declares the Lord, plans to prosper you and not to harm you, plans to give you hope and a future."
—Jeremiah 29:11

"There is a time for everything, and a season for every activity under the heavens."
—Ecclesiastes 3:1

"Trust in the Lord with all your heart and lean not on your own understanding."
—Proverbs 3:5

Consider This

Embracing change with a heart of faith can lead to incredible growth and blessings. Trust that God's plans for you are good, even when the path is uncertain.

Questions for Reflection

1. What changes are you currently facing or anticipating?

_____

_____

_____

2. How can you embrace these changes with faith in God's plan?

_____

_____

_____

3. What steps can you take to trust God more during times of change?

_____

_____

_____

Living Out Our Transformation

Step out of your comfort zone and embrace a change you've been resisting. Trust God's guidance and look for the blessings that come with new opportunities.

_____

_____

_____

_____

_____

_____

Building Deeper Connection to Transformation

- Journaling Prompt: Reflect on a past change that brought unexpected blessings. How did embracing that change grow your faith?
- Suggested Prayer: "Lord, help me to embrace the changes You bring into my life. Give me the courage to trust Your plans and see the blessings in every new opportunity. Amen."

Tomorrow's Journey

Today we embraced change. Tomorrow, we'll tackle overcoming obstacles that hinder our spiritual growth. Let's face those challenges with confidence!

DAY 4
OVERCOMING OBSTACLES

We all face obstacles in our spiritual journey. There are seasons when it feels like every step forward is met with resistance. I sometimes find myself asking God if we really have to go through this submit-and-surrender dance – again. But here's the truth: overcoming those obstacles strengthens my faith in ways I never expected.

Let me share a story. Imagine you're climbing a mountain, and as you ascend, the path gets steeper, and the air thinner. It's tough, and you might feel like giving up. But each step you take, despite the challenges, brings you closer to the summit. You discover strength and resilience you didn't know you had. You see, it's in the struggle that we grow stronger, and it's in the resistance that our faith muscles are built.

I recall a time in my life when I faced a significant obstacle. It was a period of intense personal and professional challenges. Every direction I turned seemed to present another hurdle. I was juggling the demands of a growing career and the responsibilities of family life. It felt like I was running on empty, with no end in sight. One day, after a particularly challenging meeting at work, I sat in my car, exhausted and overwhelmed. I prayed, asking God for strength and guidance. It was in that quiet moment that I felt a sense of peace wash over me, reminding me that I wasn't alone in my struggles.

As I continued to navigate through that challenging season, I noticed something incredible happening. My faith began to deepen, and my relationship with God grew stronger. I started seeing the obstacles not as barriers but as opportunities for growth. I learned to lean on God more, trusting Him to guide me through the difficulties. And just like climbing that mountain, with each step, I found myself becoming more resilient and confident in my faith.

So, if you're facing obstacles today, remember that they are not meant to defeat you but to develop you. God is using these challenges to strengthen your faith, to build your character, and to prepare you for greater things. Embrace the process, knowing that each step, no matter how difficult, is bringing you closer to the summit.

Role Models in Scripture

The story of Moses leading the Israelites out of Egypt is a testament to overcoming obstacles with God's help. From confronting Pharaoh to crossing the Red Sea and wandering in the desert, Moses faced countless challenges. Yet, he continually sought God's guidance and trusted in His power.

Imagine the scene: the Israelites trapped between the Red Sea and Pharaoh's advancing army, fear and panic spreading among the people. In the midst of this chaos, Moses stood firm and delivered a message of faith and hope. "Do not be afraid. Stand firm and you will see the deliverance the Lord will bring you today" (Exodus 14:13). This bold statement reflects Moses' unwavering faith and trust in God's deliverance, even in seemingly impossible situations.

And what happened next was nothing short of miraculous. God parted the Red Sea, providing a way of escape for the Israelites. Can you picture the amazement and awe on their faces as they walked through the sea on dry ground, walls of water standing tall on either side? This incredible event not only demonstrated God's immense power but also strengthened the faith of the Israelites. Despite their initial fear and doubt, they witnessed firsthand God's ability to overcome any obstacle.

But the journey didn't end there. The Israelites faced numerous hardships in the desert, from lack of food and water to hostile enemies and internal dissent. Each time, Moses turned to God for guidance and provision. One notable instance is when the Israelites grumbled about the lack of water at Rephidim. God instructed Moses to strike a rock, and water flowed out, providing for the people's needs (Exodus 17:1-7). This miracle reinforced the lesson that God is the ultimate provider and sustainer.

Moses' story shows us that obstacles can be overcome when we rely on God's strength and guidance. His perseverance and faith inspire us to trust God, even when the path is difficult and uncertain. Moses' life is a powerful reminder that no obstacle is too great for God to overcome. By keeping our eyes on Him and seeking His guidance, we can navigate the challenges of life with confidence and faith.

So, next time you face a daunting obstacle, remember Moses and the Red Sea. Stand firm in your faith, trust in God's deliverance, and watch as He makes a way where there seems to be no way. Just like Moses, you too can witness God's power and faithfulness in your life.

Scripture to Remember

"I can do all this through him who gives me strength."
—Philippians 4:13

"But thanks be to God! He gives us the victory through our Lord Jesus Christ."
—1 Corinthians 15:57

"The Lord will fight for you; you need only to be still."
—Exodus 14:14

Consider This

Obstacles are opportunities for God to demonstrate His power and faithfulness. Trust in His strength to overcome the challenges you face.

Questions for Reflection

1. What obstacles are hindering your spiritual growth?

    _____

    _____

    _____

2. How can you rely on God's strength to overcome these obstacles?

    _____

    _____

    _____

3. How can Moses' story inspire you to trust in God during challenging times?

    _____

    _____

    _____

Living Out Our Transformation

Identify a specific obstacle you're facing and take a step of faith to overcome it, trusting in God's power and guidance.

_____

_____

_____

_____

_____

_____

_____

Building Deeper Connection to Transformation

- Journaling Prompt: Write about a significant obstacle you've faced and how God helped you overcome it. How did this experience strengthen your faith?
- Suggested Prayer: "Lord, give me the strength to overcome the obstacles in my path. Help me to trust in Your power and guidance, knowing that You will lead me to victory. Amen."

Tomorrow's Journey

Tomorrow, we'll wrap up the week by discussing trusting God's plan. Spoiler alert: It's going to be uplifting!

DAY 5
TRUSTING GOD'S PLAN

Trusting God's plan can sometimes feel like stepping into your kids' room at night with the lights out after they've been playing with Legos all day. You know the risk of stepping on one is high, and it's a little scary. I remember a time when I had to make a big decision without knowing what the future held. It was like navigating through a dark room, feeling only the pain and danger ahead of me.

But here's the thing I've learned: trusting God is like turning on the light in that dark room. The Legos are still there, but now you can see them. You have a sense of peace because you know where to step, and the path becomes clearer. It doesn't mean the challenges disappear, but it does mean you can move forward with confidence, knowing that God is guiding you.

When we trust in God's plan, we're not promised a smooth journey without obstacles. However, we are assured that He is with us, lighting our way, and leading us to amazing outcomes that we couldn't have imagined. It's about having faith that, despite the uncertainties, God's plan is perfect and His guidance is reliable. So, let's turn on that light and step forward with faith and trust.

Role Models in Scripture

The story of Abraham is a powerful example of trusting God's plan. When God called Abraham to leave his homeland and go to a land He would show him, Abraham obeyed without hesitation. In Genesis 12:1-4, we see Abraham's immediate obedience to God's call, despite the uncertainties. His trust in God's promises was further tested when God asked him to sacrifice his son Isaac. In Genesis 22:1-18, Abraham's willingness to obey, even in this heart-wrenching command, demonstrated his profound trust in God's plan. God intervened, providing a ram as a substitute sacrifice, reaffirming His promises to Abraham.

Abraham's life is marked by moments of unwavering faith and trust in God's plan. One notable example is when God promised Abraham that he would become the father of many nations. Despite being old and childless at the time, Abraham believed God's promise. In Genesis 15:6, it says, "Abram believed the Lord, and he credited it to him as righteousness." This belief was tested many times, especially during the long wait for the promised son, Isaac. Abraham's faith journey also included moments of doubt and impatience, such as when he and Sarah tried to fulfill God's promise through their own means by having a child with Hagar. Despite these missteps, Abraham's overall narrative is one of faith and trust in God's plan.

His story encourages us to trust God's plan for our lives, even when we don't see the full picture. Trusting God means believing that His plans are good, even when our circumstances seem uncertain or challenging. Abraham's life exemplifies unwavering faith and trust in God's plan, even when the path is unclear or difficult. By following Abraham's example, we can learn to trust God more deeply, knowing that He is faithful to fulfill His promises.

Scripture to Remember

"For I know the plans I have for you, declares the Lord, plans to prosper you and not to harm you, plans to give you hope and a future."
—Jeremiah 29:11

"Trust in the Lord with all your heart and lean not on your own understanding."
—Proverbs 3:5

"And we know that in all things God works for the good of those who love him, who have been called according to his purpose."
—Romans 8:28

Consider This

Trusting God's plan involves surrendering our own desires and understanding, believing that His ways are higher and His plans are perfect.

Questions for Reflection

1. What areas of your life do you struggle to trust God with?

_____

_____

_____

2. How can you grow in your trust of God's plan for your life?

_____

_____

_____

3. What steps can you take to deepen your faith in God's promises?

_____

_____

_____

Living Out Our Transformation

Identify an area where you need to trust God more. Take a step of faith in that area, surrendering your plans to His will.

_____

_____

_____

_____

_____

_____

_____

Building Deeper Connection to Transformation

- Journaling Prompt: Reflect on a time when trusting God's plan led to unexpected blessings. How did this experience shape your faith and understanding of God's sovereignty?
- Suggested Prayer: "Lord, help me to trust Your plan for my life. Even when I don't understand, give me the faith to believe that Your ways are higher and Your plans are good. Amen."

Conclusion and Next Steps

We've covered a lot of ground this week, haven't we? Like Abraham, let's take each step with faith, knowing that God's got the roadmap—even if our GPS says, "Recalculating!" Tomorrow, we start fresh with Week 2. Get ready to dive deeper into your spiritual journey and uncover more of God's plans for you. Trust that each new day brings opportunities for growth and transformation. See you then!

WEEK 1: REFLECTION

As we come to the end of Week 1, take some time to reflect on what you have learned and how it has impacted your journey of embracing spiritual growth. Use this space to jot down your thoughts, insights, and any actions you plan to take moving forward.

Reflection Questions

1. What key insights did I gain about transformation this week?

_____

_____

_____

2. How has my understanding of spiritual growth and transformation changed or deepened?

_____

_____

_____

3. In what ways have I experienced God's presence and guidance during this week?

_____

_____

_____

4. What challenges did I face, and how did I overcome them?

_____

_____

_____

Personal Reflections

1. What specific steps can I take to continue embracing transformation in my spiritual journey?

_____

_____

_____

2. How can I incorporate the lessons learned into my daily life?

_____

_____

_____

3. Are there any areas where I still struggle with transformation? How can I address them?

_____

_____

_____

Action Plan

List three practical actions you will take in the coming week to nurture your transformation:

1. _____
   _____

2. _____
   _____

3. _____
   _____

PRAYER

Spend a few moments in prayer, asking God to help you integrate what you've learned into your daily life and to continue guiding you on your journey of transformation.

"Heavenly Father, thank You for the insights and growth I've experienced this week. Help me to carry these lessons into the coming days and to live out my transformation with confidence and trust in You. Amen."

Additional Notes

Use this space to write down any additional thoughts, prayers, or reflections you have as you conclude this week.

Preparing for Week 2

As we move into Week 2, take a moment to prepare your heart and mind for the next steps in our journey. Review the upcoming themes and consider what you hope to learn and achieve.

WEEK 2
Growing in Virtues

Welcome back! As we journey together into Week 2, we're shifting our focus to growing in the virtues that reflect Christ's character. Think of virtues as the moral superpowers that should shine in our lives as believers. They aren't just about doing good deeds; they're about becoming more like Jesus in our hearts and actions.

This week, we'll dive into virtues like patience, humility, love, faithfulness, and self-control. These are the fruits that blossom in a life rooted in Christ and nurtured by the Holy Spirit. Each day, we'll explore a different virtue, its significance, and practical ways to cultivate it in our lives. The pursuit of these virtues helps us navigate life's ups and downs with wisdom and grace, fostering deeper relationships with God and others.

Spiritual growth isn't just about avoiding sin; it's about actively growing into the person God created you to be. So, let's roll up our sleeves and dig into these virtues, understanding that it's an ongoing journey where we'll need God's help every step of the way.

Get ready for a transformative week as we embrace the virtues that draw us closer to Christ and make us more like Him in our daily lives. Let's embark on this journey with open hearts and minds, ready to grow and be transformed by His grace.

Key Themes

- Patience
- Humility
- Love
- Faithfulness
- Self-control

Anchor Scripture

"But the fruit of the Spirit is love, joy, peace, forbearance, kindness, goodness, faithfulness, gentleness and self-control. Against such things there is no law."
—Galatians 5:2223

Reflection

As we embark on this week, let's reflect on what it means to grow in the virtues that reflect Christ's character. Consider how these virtues impact our daily lives and relationships. Take time to meditate on the fruit of the Spirit and how they manifest in our actions and attitudes.

DAY 1
THE VIRTUE OF PATIENCE

When we lived in Uruguay, our family got into this routine of baking bread. I have no idea how it started, but soon we were all "expert" bread makers. Everyone but me. Why? The waiting part—letting the dough rise—felt like an eternity. As I waited for the dough to rise, I would calculate the number of times I could have walked to the corner bakery and back. I hated waiting to know if this loaf would be the one. Patience is not just passive waiting but an active trust in the process. When you break it down, baking bread is a fairly simple process with a lot of patience and flour.

This week, we begin by exploring the virtue of patience through the story of Job. Job's story is one of immense patience and faith amidst suffering. He endured great loss, yet he trusted in God's plan, even when it seemed impossible to understand. Job's patience wasn't about sitting idly by; it was about actively trusting God's goodness and timing, even in the darkest moments.

In our lives, patience is tested in various ways, whether it's waiting for a job opportunity, healing from an illness, or, like me, waiting for the dough to rise. Each moment of waiting can be an opportunity to deepen our trust in God's process and timing.

Today, let's reflect on how we can cultivate patience in our own lives. Remember, patience is not just about enduring the wait but growing through it. It's about trusting that God is at work, even when we can't see the immediate results. So, as we dive into the story of Job, let's open our hearts to the lessons of patience he teaches us and trust that, in the end, the wait will be worth it.

Role Models in Scripture

The story of Job is a profound testament to the virtue of patience. Job was a man of great wealth and integrity, described as "blameless and upright" in the eyes of God. Despite his righteousness, Job faced immense suffering when he lost his wealth, children, and health in rapid succession. Throughout his trials, Job maintained his faith in God, even when his friends and wife urged him to curse God and die. He lamented, questioned, and struggled deeply with his suffering, but he never abandoned his trust in God.

Job's patience wasn't about passive waiting; it was an active endurance and unwavering faith in God's sovereignty. His story takes us through intense dialogues with friends who misunderstand his plight, each conversation deepening Job's resolve to trust in God's ultimate plan. In the end, God speaks directly to Job, reminding him of His infinite wisdom and power. Job's restoration is profound—God restores his fortunes, giving him twice as much as he had before, including new children and an extended family.

Job's journey is a powerful reminder that patience is not merely waiting but enduring with faith and trust in God's timing and purposes, even when we don't understand His plans. His perseverance under extreme trials exemplifies a deep, unwavering faith that we are called to emulate. Job's life encourages us to remain steadfast and patient, trusting that God's plans for us are good, even in the midst of suffering.

Job's story demonstrates that true patience involves a deep, unwavering faith in God's timing and purposes, regardless of our circumstances. His journey reminds us that our trials can refine us and deepen our faith. As we reflect on Job's patience, we are encouraged to trust in God's timing, knowing that He is with us through every trial and will ultimately bring us through stronger and more faithful. Job's endurance shows that God's restoration and blessings often come after periods of intense testing and waiting. His example inspires us to hold on to our faith, trusting that God is working behind the scenes for our ultimate good and His glory.

Scripture to Remember

"Be patient, then, brothers and sisters, until the Lord's coming."
—James 5:7

"Wait for the Lord; be strong and take heart and wait for the Lord".
—Psalm 27:14

"Be joyful in hope, patient in affliction, faithful in prayer."
—Romans 12:12

Consider This

Reflect on Job's story and the depth of his patience. Consider how patience is not just about waiting but about enduring with faith and trust in God. How can you develop this kind of patience in your own life?

Day 1 The Virtue of Patience

Questions for Reflection

1. How do you typically respond to challenges and delays in your life?

_____

_____

_____

2. What steps can you take to cultivate patience, especially in difficult times?

_____

_____

_____

3. How can Job's story inspire you to trust God more deeply in your current circumstances?

_____

_____

_____

Living Out Our Transformation

Identify an area in your life where you need more patience. Spend time in prayer, asking God to help you develop patience and trust in His timing.

_____

_____

_____

_____

_____

_____

Building Deeper Connection to Transformation

- Journaling Prompt: Reflect on a time when you had to wait patiently for something important. How did this experience shape your faith and patience?
- Suggested Prayer: "Heavenly Father, thank You for the example of Job and his patience. Help me to develop patience in my own life, trusting in Your timing and plan. Strengthen my faith and endurance in all circumstances. Amen."

Tomorrow's Journey

Just like waiting for bread to rise, growing in patience can feel slow and tedious. But remember, the end result is worth the wait. Tomorrow, we'll dive into the virtue of humility, so let's knead this lesson of patience into our hearts today.

DAY 2
THE VIRTUE OF HUMILITY

Ever had a moment where you thought you had everything figured out, only to realize you needed help? When my kids were little, I swore life would continue uninterrupted and that all that was needed was a little better time management. Yeah... so I thought until the day the bottom of a trash bag full of dirty diapers broke open, and diapers rained down my legs, over my shoes, and bounced their way to the bottom of the stairs. It was in that moment I forfeited any sense of real control. Humility often starts with such realizations.

Humility isn't just about recognizing our limitations; it's about embracing them and understanding that we don't have to do everything on our own. I remember trying to juggle work, family, and personal goals, believing I could handle it all. But life has a way of reminding us that we need help. It's in those humbling moments we realize the importance of relying on others and, most importantly, on God.

Humility is also about seeing the value in others and their contributions. It's easy to get caught up in our achievements and forget that we are part of a larger community. When we humble ourselves, we open our hearts to learning from others and recognizing that everyone has something valuable to offer. Today, as we delve into the virtue of humility through the story of Moses, let's reflect on how we can embrace humility in our own lives.

Role Models in Scripture

The story of Moses offers a compelling example of humility. Born a Hebrew slave but raised in the Egyptian royal household, Moses had a unique position of privilege and power. However, after killing an Egyptian taskmaster, he fled to the desert, becoming a shepherd. When God called him from the burning bush to lead the Israelites out of Egypt, Moses initially resisted, expressing his feelings of inadequacy and unworthiness. Despite his doubts, Moses obeyed God's call, relying on God's strength rather than his own.

Throughout the journey, Moses demonstrated humility by continually seeking God's guidance and giving Him the glory for their victories. His humility allowed him to lead effectively, acknowledging that it was God's power at work, not his own. Moses' story illustrates that true humility involves recognizing our dependence on God and giving Him the glory in all things, even when we are placed in positions of leadership or face daunting challenges.

Moses' humility is evident in how he handled the complaints and rebellions of the Israelites. Instead of asserting his authority harshly, he often turned to God in prayer, seeking divine wisdom and intervention. This reliance on God over his own abilities exemplifies the essence of humility. Moses knew that without God's guidance, he could not lead the people effectively.

One of the most striking moments of Moses' humility is seen when God threatened to destroy the Israelites for their disobedience, and Moses interceded on their behalf, pleading with God to spare them. Moses' willingness to stand in the gap for his people, despite their flaws, shows his selfless nature and deep reliance on God's mercy.

Moses' story teaches us that humility is about recognizing our limitations and God's limitless power. It's about stepping back and allowing God to lead, even when we are in positions of authority.

His life challenges us to cultivate humility by acknowledging our dependence on God and giving Him the glory in all things.

Scripture to Remember

"Now Moses was a very humble man, more humble than anyone else on the face of the earth."
—Numbers 12:3

"Do nothing out of selfish ambition or vain conceit. Rather, in humility value others above yourselves."
—Philippians 2:3

"Humble yourselves before the Lord, and he will lift you up."
—James 4:10

Consider This

Reflect on Moses' journey and his humility in accepting God's call. Consider how true humility involves recognizing our dependence on God and giving Him the glory in all things. How can you develop a humble heart and mindset?

Questions for Reflection

1. How do you respond when faced with tasks or challenges that seem beyond your abilities?

_____

_____

_____

2. In what areas of your life can you practice more humility?

_____

_____

_____

3. How can you rely more on God's strength rather than your own?

_____

_____

_____

Living Out Our Transformation

Identify one way you can practice humility today. Spend time in prayer, asking God to help you develop a humble heart and to give Him the glory in all things.

_____

_____

_____

_____

_____

_____

_____

Building Deeper Connection to Transformation

*   Journaling Prompt: Reflect on a time when you had to rely on someone else's help. How did it feel to admit you needed assistance? What did you learn from that experience about humility?

- Suggested Prayer: "Heavenly Father, thank You for the example of Moses and his humility. Help me to develop humility in my own life, recognizing my dependence on You and giving You the glory in all things. Strengthen my faith and reliance on Your strength. Amen."

Tomorrow's Journey

Being humble is like learning to dance in a group—you've got to follow the lead and work together. Tomorrow, we'll explore the virtue of love, so let's step gracefully into humility today.

DAY 3
THE VIRTUE OF LOVE

Imagine a world where everyone loved their neighbors as themselves and used their turn signals. Sounds like a dream, right? Or at a minimum a far-off land that no one has invited you to. I recall a moment when I witnessed an act of love that truly warmed my heart. It was a simple gesture—someone helping an elderly lady cross the street during a particularly chaotic rush hour. It wasn't just about getting her to the other side safely; it was the smile and kind words exchanged that left a lasting impression on me. These small acts of love can transform the ordinary into the extraordinary, showing us the profound impact love can have in our daily lives.

Love is not just about grand gestures; it's about the everyday actions that reflect God's heart. It's about how we treat the people we encounter daily, from our family and friends to the strangers we pass by on the street. When we choose to love, we reflect God's love and bring a piece of heaven to earth.

Today, we're diving into the virtue of love through the story of the Good Samaritan. This parable teaches us about the power of love in action and challenges us to extend our compassion beyond our comfort zones. It's easy to love those who love us back, but the true test of love is how we treat those who may not be easy to love. The Good Samaritan showed love and kindness to a stranger, crossing cultural and social boundaries to help someone in need.

As we explore this story, let's open our hearts to the transformative power of love. Let's challenge ourselves to look for opportunities to show love in our daily lives, even when it's inconvenient or uncomfortable. In doing so, we can become vessels of God's love, making a tangible difference in the world around us.

Role Models in Scripture

The story of the Good Samaritan is one of the most profound illustrations of love in action. Jesus told this parable to a lawyer who asked, "And who is my neighbor?" In the story, a man is attacked by robbers and left for dead. A priest and a Levite, both religious figures, pass by without helping. But a Samaritan, considered an enemy by the Jews, stops to help the injured man. He bandages his wounds, takes him to an inn, and pays for his care. The Samaritan's actions demonstrate true love and compassion, crossing cultural and religious boundaries. This parable teaches us that love is not just a feeling but an action, a commitment to care for others, even those we might consider our enemies. It challenges us to move beyond our prejudices and self-centeredness to extend love and kindness to everyone in need.

In the context of the cultural animosity between Jews and Samaritans, the actions of the Good Samaritan are even more remarkable. He not only provided immediate first aid but also ensured the injured man's continued care by paying the innkeeper. The Samaritan's willingness to go out of his way, financially and physically, to care for a stranger underscore the depth of his compassion and love.

The parable challenges us to reflect on how we define our neighbor. It expands the concept of neighbor to include anyone who is in need, regardless of their background, beliefs, or circumstances. This radical love breaks down barriers and calls us to act with compassion and mercy, just as the Samaritan did.

The Good Samaritan's story also highlights the importance of action in demonstrating love. It's not enough to feel compassion; we must also act on it. True love is seen in our willingness to step into uncomfortable situations, to help those who may not be able to repay us, and to extend grace and kindness without expecting anything in return.

As we reflect on the parable of the Good Samaritan, we are challenged to consider how we can embody this selfless, action-oriented love in our own lives. It calls us to look beyond our comfort zones and to love others with the same generosity and compassion that the Samaritan showed.

Scripture to Remember

"A new command I give you: Love one another. As I have loved you, so you must love one another."
—John 13:34

"Love is patient, love is kind. It does not envy, it does not boast, it is not proud."
—1 Corinthians 13:4

"Dear friends, let us love one another, for love comes from God."
—1 John 4:7

Consider This

Reflect on the parable of the Good Samaritan and the example of love in action. Consider how true love involves selflessness and compassion, extending care to others regardless of who they are. How can you demonstrate thiskind of love in your life?

Questions for Reflection

1. How do you currently show love and compassion to others?

_____

_____

_____

2. In what ways can you extend love to those who are difficult to love?

_____

_____

_____

3. What practical steps can you take to demonstrate love in action in your daily life?

_____

_____

_____

Living Out Our Transformation

Identify one way you can show love and compassion to someone today. Spend time in prayer, asking God to help you love others as He loves you.

_____

_____

_____

_____

_____

_____

_____

Building Deeper Connection to Transformation

- Journaling Prompt: Reflect on a time when you showed or received unexpected love. How did it impact you or the other person? What does this teach you about the transformative power of love?
- Suggested Prayer: "Heavenly Father, thank You for the example of the Good Samaritan and his love in action. Help me to demonstrate true love and compassion in my life, extending care to others regardless of who they are. Strengthen my heart to love as You love. Amen."

Tomorrow's Journey

Loving others, especially those who are difficult to love, can be challenging. But just like a warm hug on a cold day, it can be incredibly comforting and transformative. Tomorrow, we'll look at the virtue of faithfulness, so let's wrap ourselves in love today.

DAY 4
THE VIRTUE OF
FAITHFULNESS

Faithfulness is like that one friend who always shows up, even when everyone else bails. You know, the friend who helps you move and still buys you pizza afterward. It's that dependable, unwavering presence that makes all the difference. Today, let's dive into the story of Daniel in the lion's den to understand the true essence of faithfulness.

Imagine you're in a room filled with your childhood toys. Among all the flashy new gadgets, there's that one beloved teddy bear, worn and a bit scruffy, but always there for you. Faithfulness is that teddy bear—a constant, reassuring presence no matter what comes your way. It's about showing up, standing firm, and being reliable even when life throws curveballs.

Faithfulness isn't just about the big, grand gestures. It's about the little, everyday actions that build trust and reliability over time. It's like brushing your teeth every morning—simple, routine, but essential. Without it, things quickly go downhill. Today, we're going to explore how Daniel's unwavering faithfulness, even in the face of lions, serves as a powerful example for us all.

Prepare to be inspired by Daniel's incredible journey. His story isn't just about surviving a night with some big cats; it's about the steadfast faith and trust in God that kept him strong. As we unpack this story, think about the areas in your life where you can show a little more faithfulness and trust in God's plan.

Role Models in Scripture

The story of Daniel in the lion's den is a powerful example of faithfulness. Daniel, a man of unwavering faith, continued to pray to God despite a decree from King Darius that prohibited prayer to anyone except the king. When Daniel was discovered praying, he was thrown into the lion's den. However, God protected him, and he emerged unharmed the next morning. Daniel's faithfulness in the face of danger not only preserved his life but also led King Darius to issue a decree honoring Daniel's God.

Daniel's faithfulness is seen in his consistent prayer life. He prayed three times a day, facing Jerusalem, even when it became illegal. His commitment to his spiritual discipline was unshaken by the threat of death. This unwavering dedication to God, despite the potential consequences, is a testament to his deep faith and trust in God's protection and provision.

The impact of Daniel's faithfulness extended beyond his personal safety. His miraculous deliverance from the lion's den caused King Darius to recognize the power and sovereignty of Daniel's God. This led to a royal decree that honored God throughout the kingdom, demonstrating how one person's faithfulness can influence and inspire others.

Daniel's story teaches us that faithfulness means remaining steadfast in our devotion to God, even when it's risky or unpopular. His unwavering commitment to God serves as a powerful reminder that our faithfulness can influence others and bring glory to God. It challenges us to remain committed to our spiritual disciplines and trust in God's protection and provision, regardless of the circumstances.

Daniel's life encourages us to cultivate a consistent and unwavering faith, trusting that God is always with us and will honor our commitment to Him. His story reminds us that faithfulness in our relationship with God is a powerful testimony to others and can lead to significant spiritual impact.

Scripture to Remember

"Now it is required that those who have been given a trust must prove faithful."
—1 Corinthians 4:2

"Let us hold unswervingly to the hope we profess, for he who promised is faithful."
—Hebrews 10:23

"Be faithful, even to the point of death, and I will give you life as your victor's crown."
—Revelation 2:10

Consider This

Reflect on Daniel's unwavering faithfulness to God, even in the face of danger. Consider how you can develop and maintain faithfulness in your own life. What does it mean to be faithful in your commitments and relationships?

Questions for Reflection

1. How can you demonstrate faithfulness in your relationship with God?

_____

_____

_____

2. In what areas of your life can you show greater faithfulness and commitment?

_____

_____

_____

3. How does Daniel's example inspire you to remain steadfast in your faith, even when faced with challenges?

_____

_____

_____

Living Out Our Transformation

Identify one area where you need to demonstrate greater faithfulness. Spend time in prayer, asking God to help you remain steadfast in your commitments and relationships.

_____

_____

_____

_____

_____

_____

_____

Building Deeper Connection to Transformation

- Journaling Prompt: Reflect on a time when you experienced someone's faithfulness. How did it impact you? How can you emulate this faithfulness in your own life?
- Suggested Prayer: "Heavenly Father, thank You for the example of Daniel and his unwavering faithfulness. Help me to develop and maintain faithfulness in my own life, remaining steadfast in my devotion to You. Strengthen my commitment to my faith and relationships. Amen."

Tomorrow's Journey

Faithfulness is like a sturdy bridge—strong, reliable, and built to last. Tomorrow, we'll explore the virtue of self-control, so let's build on the foundation of faithfulness today.

DAY 5
THE VIRTUE OF
SELF-CONTROL

Imagine having a box of your favorite black-and-white cookies on the table and resisting the urge to eat them all in one sitting. That's a bit like self-control, isn't it? Now, picture this: my client sent me a box of the most delicious black-and-white cookies. They were calling my name. I thought, "I'll just have one." An hour later, the box was empty, and I had crumbs all over me. Self-control? More like self-destruct!

Now, let's talk about Joseph. He had a far more serious test of self-control. Sold into slavery by his jealous brothers and taken to Egypt, Joseph found himself in the house of Potiphar, an Egyptian official. Despite his circumstances, Joseph remained faithful and diligent, earning Potiphar's trust. Things took a turn when Potiphar's wife tried to seduce him. Unlike my cookie fiasco, Joseph's self-control was rock solid. He refused her advances, saying, "How could I do such a wicked thing and sin against God?" (Genesis 39:9).

Joseph's self-control wasn't just about resisting temptation; it was about staying true to his values and honoring God. Even when he was unjustly thrown into prison for his refusal, Joseph maintained his integrity. His ability to exercise self-control in such a challenging situation eventually led to his rise as a powerful leader in Egypt.

So, while resisting cookies is tough, Joseph shows us that self-control is essential in staying true to our values and faith, even when the pressure is on. Today, let's learn from Joseph and strive to master the art of self-control, one black-and-white cookie at a time!

Role Models in Scripture

The story of Joseph provides a powerful example of self-control. Sold into slavery by his brothers and later imprisoned unjustly, Joseph faced numerous challenges and temptations. Despite these circumstances, he remained faithful to God. When Potiphar's wife tried to seduce him, Joseph exercised remarkable self-control and fled from the situation, even though it led to his imprisonment. Throughout his trials, Joseph consistently demonstrated self-control, trusting in God's plan for his life. His self-discipline eventually led to his rise to power in Egypt, where he saved many from famine. Joseph's story teaches us that self-control involves trusting God's plan and resisting temptations, even when it's difficult. His example encourages us to rely on God's strength to maintain self-control in our own lives.

Joseph's life is a testament to the power of self-control in overcoming adversity. Despite being betrayed by his own brothers and facing numerous injustices, Joseph did not allow bitterness or anger to take root in his heart. His ability to control his emotions and actions in the face of severe trials showcases a deep trust in God's sovereignty and timing.

One of the most notable aspects of Joseph's story is his encounter with Potiphar's wife. Her persistent attempts to seduce him were met with Joseph's firm refusal and determination to maintain his integrity. His statement, "How then can I do this great wickedness and sin against God?" (Genesis 39:9), reflects his commitment to self-control and his reverence for God.

Joseph's journey from a slave to the second-in-command in Egypt highlights how self-control and faithfulness can lead to God's favor and blessings. His ability to interpret Pharaoh's dreams and his wise management during the years of plenty and famine saved countless lives, including those of his own family who had betrayed him.

Joseph's forgiveness of his brothers further exemplifies his self-control. Instead of seeking revenge, he recognized God's hand in his life's events and chose to forgive and provide for his family. His story challenges us to exercise self-control in our responses to life's challenges, trusting that God is working for our good.

Scripture to Remember

"But the fruit of the Spirit is love, joy, peace, forbearance, kindness, goodness, faithfulness, gentleness and self-control."
—Galatians 5:2223

"For the Spirit God gave us does not make us timid, but gives us power, love and self-discipline."
—2 Timothy 1:7

"Everyone who competes in the games goes into strict training. They do it to get a crown that will not last, but we do it to get a crown that will last forever."
—1 Corinthians 9:25

Consider This

Reflect on Joseph's story and his remarkable self-control in the face of temptation. Consider how self-control is essential in resisting temptations and following God's plan. How can you develop self-control in your daily life?

Questions for Reflection

1. How can you practice self-control in your daily life?

   _____

   _____

   _____

2. What steps can you take to overcome areas where you lack self-control?

   _____

   _____

   _____

3. How does trusting in God help you maintain self-control?

   _____

   _____

   _____

4. In what situations do you find it hardest to exercise self-control, and how can you prepare to face those challenges?

   _____

   _____

   _____

Living Out Our Transformation

Identify one area where you need to develop greater self-control. Spend time in prayer, asking God to help you exercise self-control and rely on His strength.

_____

_____

_____

_____

_____

_____

_____

Building Deeper Connection to Transformation

- Journaling Prompt: Reflect on a time when you exercised self-control in a challenging situation. How did it feel? What did you learn from that experience?
- Suggested Prayer: "Heavenly Father, thank You for the example of Joseph and his remarkable self-control. Help me to develop self-control in my own life, particularly in areas where I struggle. Strengthen my resolve and reliance on Your strength. Amen."

Self-control is like having a well-guarded treasure—precious and protected. As we wrap up this week, let's hold on to these virtues and let them shape our lives. Ready for Week 3? Let's keep growing together!

WEEK 2 REFLECTION

As we come to the end of Week 2, take some time to reflect on what you have learned and how it has impacted your spiritual growth. Use this space to jot down your thoughts, insights, and any actions you plan to take moving forward.

Reflection Questions

1. What key insights did I gain about growing in virtues this week?

_____

_____

_____

2. How has my understanding of spiritual virtues changed or deepened?

_____

_____

_____

3. In what ways have I experienced God's presence and guidance during this week?

_____

_____

_____

4. What challenges did I face, and how did I overcome them?

_____

_____

_____

Personal Reflections

1. What specific steps can I take to continue growing in virtues?

_____

_____

_____

2. How can I incorporate the lessons learned into my daily life?

_____

_____

_____

3. Are there any areas where I still struggle with these virtues? How can I address them?

_____

_____

_____

Action Plan

List three practical actions you will take in the coming week to nurture your spiritual growth.

1. _____
_____

2. _____
_____

3. _____
_____

PRAYER

Spend a few moments in prayer, asking God to help you integrate what you've learned into your daily life and to continue guiding you on your spiritual journey.

"Heavenly Father, thank You for the insights and growth I've experienced this week. Help me to carry these lessons into the coming days and to live out my faith with confidence and trust in You. Amen."

Additional Notes

Use this space to write down any additional thoughts, prayers, or reflections you have as you conclude this week.

_____

_____

_____

_____

_____

_____

Preparing for Week 3

As we move into Week 3, take a moment to prepare your heart and mind for the next steps in our journey. Review the upcoming themes and consider what you hope to learn and achieve.

WEEK 3
Embracing Your Role
as a
Leader and Light

Hey there, fellow traveler! If you're anything like me, the idea of being a leader or a light in this world can sometimes feel overwhelming. We might think that leadership is reserved for those with fancy titles or that shining brightly means having it all together. But this week, we're going to discover that leadership in God's kingdom is about servanthood, humility, and reflecting Christ's light in our everyday actions.

This final week of our journey focuses on embracing the roles God has for us as leaders, lights in the world, and His beloved. We'll explore how to set an example for others, be friends of Jesus, and shine brightly in a world that desperately needs His light. This week will empower us to walk boldly in the identity God has given us.

Let's dive into the heart of leadership and light, understanding that it's not about perfection but about showing up with love, grace, and authenticity. As we go through this week, let's remind ourselves that we're in this together, supporting and encouraging each other as we grow in our roles.

Key Themes

- A Leader of Men
- The Light of the World
- His Beloved

Anchor Scripture

"You are the light of the world. A town built on a hill cannot be hidden."
—Matthew 5:14

Reflection

Consider how you can be a light in your community through your actions and words. Reflect on the comfort and strength from knowing you are His beloved and let this assurance help you lead and inspire others. Look for daily opportunities to show kindness, offer encouragement, and stand up for what is right.

As we embark on this final week, let's commit to being intentional as leaders and lights. Make a list of practical ways to reflect Christ's light in your daily interactions. Reach out to someone who needs encouragement, take a stand for justice, or be a friend to someone who is lonely. Embrace your identity as God's beloved and lead with love, knowing that your actions, big or small, can inspire and uplift those around you.

DAY 1
THE ROLE OF A LEADER

Think about the last time you had to step up and lead, whether it was organizing a family gathering or guiding a team project at work. You might have felt unsure, telling yourself or others that you were not a leader. But leadership comes in many forms, and sometimes it sneaks up on us in the most unexpected ways.

John C. Maxwell teaches that leadership is not about titles, positions, or flowcharts. It's about one life influencing another. It's the simple actions of guidance and support that truly define a leader. When Moses was called by God to lead the Israelites out of Egypt, he didn't see himself as a leader. He doubted his abilities and questioned God's choice. Yet, through God's guidance and his own willingness to step forward, Moses became one of the greatest leaders in history.

Leadership is often about being willing to step into roles that challenge us, to influence others positively, and to trust that we can grow into the responsibilities we are given. Whether it's through offering a listening ear, making a tough decision, or simply being there for someone in need, every act of leadership makes a difference.

Today, we'll explore what it means to be a leader through the life of Moses, understanding that true leadership is about influence, service, and the courage to step up, even when we feel inadequate.

Role Models in Scripture

Moses is one of the most compelling examples of leadership in the Bible. Born a Hebrew slave but raised in the Egyptian royal household, Moses had a unique upbringing that prepared him for his future role. Despite his privileged position, Moses' journey was marked by significant challenges and a profound sense of inadequacy.

When Moses encountered God in the burning bush, he was called to lead the Israelites out of Egypt. Initially, Moses was reluctant, expressing his doubts and fears. He questioned his ability to speak and lead, saying, "Who am I that I should go to Pharaoh and bring the Israelites out of Egypt?" (Exodus 3:11). Despite his hesitation, God reassured Moses, promising to be with him and to empower him for the task ahead.

Moses' leadership was characterized by his deep reliance on God. He frequently sought God's guidance and strength, especially during difficult times. For instance, when the Israelites faced the Red Sea with the Egyptian army closing in, Moses trusted in God's deliverance. God parted the sea, allowing the Israelites to escape and demonstrating His power through Moses' leadership.

Throughout their journey in the wilderness, Moses faced numerous challenges, including complaints and rebellions from the people. Yet, he remained steadfast, interceding for the Israelites and leading them with patience and humility. One of the most striking moments of Moses' leadership was when he received the Ten Commandments on Mount Sinai. This event not only provided the Israelites with a moral and spiritual foundation but also solidified Moses' role as a mediator between God and His people.

Moses' story teaches us that true leadership involves humility, reliance on God, and a willingness to serve others. His life reminds us that God doesn't call the equipped; He equips the called. Moses' journey from a hesitant leader to a revered prophet illustrates that with God's help, we can overcome our insecurities and lead with confidence and faith.

Scripture to Remember

"The Lord is my strength and my defense; he has become my salvation."
—Exodus 15:2

"The Lord replied, 'My Presence will go with you, and I will give you rest.'"
—Exodus 33:14

"By faith Moses, when he had grown up, refused to be known as the son of Pharaoh's daughter."
—Hebrews 11:24

Consider This

Reflect on Moses' journey from hesitant follower to strong leader. Think about how his relationship with God enabled him to lead effectively. Spend time journaling about any leadership roles God may be calling you to and how you can rely on His strength to fulfill them.

Questions for Reflection

1. What leadership roles do you feel God is calling you to?

_____

_____

_____

2. How can you rely on God's strength and wisdom in your leadership?

_____

_____

_____

3. In what ways can you demonstrate humility and reliance on God in your leadership?

_____

_____

_____

4. How can Moses' example inspire you to embrace your own leadership journey?

_____

_____

_____

Living Out Our Transformation

Identify one area where you can step into a leadership role, trusting God to guide and empower you.

_____

_____

_____

_____

_____

_____

_____

Building Deeper Connection to Transformation

- Journaling Prompt: Reflect on a time when you had to lead in a challenging situation. How did you rely on God's strength and guidance?
- Suggested Prayer: "Lord, help me to lead with humility and trust in Your guidance. Equip me to serve others and reflect Your love in all I do. Amen."

Tomorrow's Journey

Leadership isn't about having all the answers; it's about being willing to step up and trust God to guide you. Tomorrow, we'll explore what it means to be the light of the world. So let's shine brightly in our leadership today.

DAY 2
THE LIGHT OF THE WORLD

Have you ever stumbled around in the dark, feeling completely lost, only to find relief when someone turned on a light? It's an incredible feeling, isn't it? That's what being the light of the world is like—bringing clarity, hope, and guidance to those who are struggling in darkness. Imagine walking through a pitch-black room and then someone flips the switch, suddenly everything becomes clear. That's the kind of impact we're called to have in this world. Today, we're going to explore what it means to be that light through a personal story about bringing light to others.

I remember a time when I was new to my job, trying to navigate the ins and outs of the office. Everything felt so overwhelming. Then, one of my colleagues, Sarah, took the time to show me around, explain the processes, and introduce me to others. She didn't have to do it, but her kindness and guidance were like a light in a dark room for me. Sarah's actions made a world of difference. She didn't just tell me what to do—she walked with me through the challenges, offered support, and made me feel welcome and valued. Her light shone brightly in a time when I needed it most.

Being a light in the world isn't about having all the answers or being perfect. It's about showing up, being present, and letting your kindness and compassion shine through. It's about offering a kind word, a helping hand, or a listening ear. It's about being courageous in our kindness, even when we're unsure of the outcome.

Think about the power of a single flashlight during a power outage. It might seem small, but it can light up the entire room and provide comfort and direction. That's what Sarah did for me, and that's what we can do for others. Just like Sarah, we have the opportunity to shine brightly in our families, workplaces, and communities.

So, let's take this example to heart. Let's strive to be a beacon of hope and guidance, shining our light into every dark corner we encounter. And remember, no matter how small our light might seem, it has the power to transform the world around us.

Role Models in Scripture

Deborah, a prophetess and judge of Israel, is a remarkable example of what it means to be a light in the world. At a time when female leaders were rare, Deborah's wisdom and courage shone brightly, guiding the nation of Israel through a period of turmoil and oppression.

Deborah held court under the Palm of Deborah, where the Israelites came to her for judgment. She was not only a judge but also a military leader. When the Israelites faced oppression from King Jabin of Canaan, Deborah called Barak to lead the army against Sisera, the commander of Jabin's army. Despite Barak's hesitance and insistence that Deborah accompany him into battle, she agreed, demonstrating her leadership and faith.

During the battle, Deborah's presence and encouragement were vital to the morale of the troops. Her faith in God's deliverance inspired confidence in the Israelite soldiers. The victory over Sisera's forces was a testament to Deborah's leadership and her unwavering trust in God.

Deborah's story illustrates the power of being a light in the world through faith and action. Her leadership brought about not only a military victory but also a spiritual awakening among the people. Following the battle, Deborah and Barak sang a song of victory, celebrating God's deliverance and reminding the Israelites of His faithfulness.

Deborah's life teaches us that being a light involves stepping into our roles with confidence and trust in God. Her courage and wisdom were not her own but were gifts from God, which she used to lead and inspire others. Deborah's story encourages us to let our light shine by using our God-given gifts and trusting in His strength, even when we face opposition or uncertainty.

Scripture to Remember

"You are the light of the world. A town built on a hill cannot be hidden."
—Matthew 5:14

"The light shines in the darkness, and the darkness has not overcome it."
—John 1:5

"For you were once darkness, but now you are light in the Lord. Live as children of light."
—Ephesians 5:8

Consider This

Reflect on Deborah's role as a light in a dark time. Consider how her faith and leadership brought about victory for Israel. Spend time journaling about how you can be a light in your community, using your gifts and influence to make a positive impact.

Questions for Reflection

1. How can you be a light in your community?

    _____

    _____

    _____

2. What gifts and influence can you use to bring about God's purposes?

    _____

    _____

    _____

3. In what specific situations have you felt called to be a light, and how did you respond?

    _____

    _____

    _____

Living Out Our Transformation

Identify one specific way you can shine your light in your community this week.

_____

_____

_____

_____

_____

_____

Building Deeper Connection to Transformation

- **Journaling Prompt:** Reflect on a time when you felt called to be a light in a difficult situation. How did God use you to bring hope and clarity?
- **Suggested Prayer:** "Lord, help me to be a light in the world, shining Your love and truth in all I do. Use my gifts and influence to bring glory to Your name. Amen."

Tomorrow's Journey

Being a light means bringing hope and clarity to those around us. Tomorrow, we'll explore what it means to be God's beloved. Let's shine brightly today and spread God's love.

DAY 3
HIS BELOVED

Have you ever received a letter or an email that made you feel incredibly cherished? Those words that remind you of your worth and how deeply you are appreciated can transform your entire day. Now, imagine feeling that sense of being cherished and loved every single day, not just by people but by God Himself. Knowing that we are God's beloved can transform our lives in profound ways. Today, we reflect on being His beloved through the story of Mary, the mother of Jesus.

One of the most significant aspects of being God's beloved is understanding that His love for us is unconditional and everlasting. It's not based on our performance or our ability to earn it, but purely on His grace. This can be a difficult concept to grasp, especially in a world where love often feels conditional. But God's love is different; it's steadfast, unwavering, and always available to us. Embracing this truth can change how we view ourselves and how we navigate the ups and downs of life.

When we truly accept our identity as God's beloved, it impacts every area of our lives. It gives us the confidence to face challenges, the courage to pursue our calling, and the peace to rest in His promises. Just like Mary, who embraced her role in God's plan with humility and faith, we too can find strength and purpose in knowing we are loved by our Creator.

Role Models in Scripture

Mary, the mother of Jesus, is a profound example of what it means to be God's beloved. Chosen by God to bear His Son, Mary's journey was marked by faith, obedience, and an unwavering trust in God's plan. Her story begins with an extraordinary encounter with the angel Gabriel, who announced that she would conceive and bear a son, Jesus.

Despite the fear and uncertainty that this news brought, Mary responded with remarkable faith and humility. She said, "I am the Lord's servant. May your word to me be fulfilled" (Luke 1:38). This response exemplifies her deep trust in God and her willingness to embrace His will, even when it meant facing societal judgment and personal sacrifice.

Throughout her life, Mary's identity as God's beloved was evident in her actions and attitudes. From the moment of Jesus' birth in a humble stable to His crucifixion on the cross, Mary remained steadfast in her faith and devotion. She pondered the words of the shepherds and wise men in her heart, nurtured Jesus as He grew, and stood by Him during His ministry, even when it led to His ultimate sacrifice.

One of the most poignant moments in Mary's story is when she stood at the foot of the cross, watching her beloved Son suffer and die. Despite the immense pain and sorrow, Mary's faith did not waver. Her presence at the crucifixion and her role in the early church highlight her enduring commitment to God's plan and her unwavering trust in His promises.

Mary's story teaches us that being God's beloved means embracing His plan for our lives with faith and obedience. It involves trusting Him, even when we face challenges and uncertainties. Mary's life encourages us to find our identity in God's love and to live out that identity with courage and faithfulness.

Scripture to Remember

"See what great love the Father has lavished on us, that we should be called children of God! And that is what we are!"
—1 John 3:1

"I have loved you with an everlasting love; I have drawn you with unfailing kindness."
—Jeremiah 31:3

"The Lord your God is with you, the Mighty Warrior who saves. He will take great delight in you; in his love he will no longer rebuke you, but will rejoice over you with singing."
—Zephaniah 3:17

Consider This

Reflect on Mary's journey as God's beloved and her unwavering faith and obedience. Think about how her trust in God's plan enabled her to fulfill her unique role. Spend time journaling about how you can embrace your identity as God's beloved and trust Him in your journey.

Questions for Reflection

1. What does it mean to you to be God's beloved?

   _____

   _____

   _____

2. How can you trust God's plan for your life, even in difficult times?

   _____

   _____

   _____

3. In what ways can you live out your identity as God's beloved in your daily actions?

   _____

   _____

   _____

Living Out Our Transformation

Write a prayer expressing your trust in God's plan and your commitment to living as His beloved.

_____

_____

_____

_____

_____

_____

_____

Building Deeper Connection to Transformation

- Journaling Prompt: Reflect on a time when knowing you are God's beloved gave you strength and comfort. How did this assurance impact your actions and decisions?
- Suggested Prayer: "Heavenly Father, thank You for loving me with an everlasting love. Help me to embrace my identity as Your beloved and to trust Your plan for my life. Amen."

Tomorrow's Journey

Being God's beloved gives us the strength and comfort to face life's challenges. Tomorrow, we'll explore the importance of leading with humility. Let's embrace our identity in God's love today. Being God's beloved gives us the strength and comfort to face life's challenges. Tomorrow, we'll explore the importance of leading with humility. Let's embrace our identity in God's love today.

Top of Form

Bottom of Form

DAY 4
LEADING WITH HUMILITY

There once was a father and son who often found themselves at odds. The son, full of youthful vigor and a desire to prove himself, constantly challenged his father's wisdom. Every task, from fixing a broken fence to making a family decision, became a battleground. The son was determined to show he had all the answers, but time and time again, his efforts fell short. One summer, they decided to build a treehouse together. The son, convinced he could handle it on his own, dismissed his father's offers of help and guidance. He eagerly started the project, envisioning a grand masterpiece. But as the days went by, he realized he had underestimated the complexity of the task. The materials didn't fit together as he had imagined, and the treehouse was far from stable. Frustration and disappointment set in.

It wasn't until the son faced the inevitable collapse of his half-built treehouse that he swallowed his pride and turned to his father for guidance. With humility, he admitted he didn't know everything and asked for his father's help. His father, with a gentle smile, stepped in and together, they rebuilt the treehouse. This time, it stood tall and strong, a symbol of their collaborative effort and mutual respect.

This story mirrors our own lives when we realize the power of leading with humility. Leading with humility means recognizing our limitations and trusting in God's strength. Today, let's explore humility through the life of Nehemiah. His story shows us that we don't need to have all the answers; we just need to have faith and rely on God's guidance.

Role Models in Scripture

Nehemiah, a humble cupbearer to the king, became a great leader through his reliance on God. When Nehemiah heard about the ruined state of Jerusalem's walls, he was deeply moved and felt a divine call to rebuild them. His story begins in the Persian palace, where he served King Artaxerxes. Despite his comfortable position, Nehemiah's heart was with his people in Jerusalem.

Upon hearing the news of Jerusalem's desolation, Nehemiah immediately turned to God in prayer and fasting. He confessed the sins of Israel and sought God's favor in approaching the king for permission to rebuild the walls. When granted this permission, Nehemiah traveled to Jerusalem and began the daunting task of rebuilding.

Nehemiah's leadership was marked by humility and dependence on God. He faced fierce opposition from surrounding enemies who mocked and threatened the workers. Despite these challenges, Nehemiah's trust in God remained unwavering. He encouraged the people, saying, "Don't be afraid of them. Remember the Lord, who is great and awesome, and fight for your families, your sons, and your daughters, your wives, and your homes" (Nehemiah 4:14).

Throughout the rebuilding process, Nehemiah demonstrated humility by continuously seeking God's guidance. He knew that the task was beyond his ability and that only through God's strength and favor could the walls be rebuilt. Nehemiah's humility and dedication inspired the people to work together, and they completed the wall in just 52 days.

Nehemiah's story teaches us that true leadership involves serving others and relying on God's strength. His humility allowed him to lead effectively, acknowledging that it was God's power at work, not his own. Nehemiah's life reminds us that when we lead with humility and trust in God, we can accomplish great things for His glory.

Scripture to Remember

"Humble yourselves before the Lord, and he will lift you up."
— James 4:10

"Do nothing out of selfish ambition or vain conceit. Rather, in humility value others above yourselves."
—Philippians 2:3

"For all those who exalt themselves will be humbled, and those who humble themselves will be exalted."
—Luke 14:11

Consider This

Reflect on Nehemiah's humble leadership and his dependence on God. Consider how his humility and dedication led to the successful rebuilding of Jerusalem's walls. Spend time journaling about how you can lead with humility and serve others, relying on God's strength.

Questions for Reflection

1. How can you lead with humility in your life?

    _____

    _____

    _____

2. In what areas do you need to rely more on God's strength?

    _____

    _____

    _____

3. What steps can you take to practice humility in your daily interactions?

    _____

    _____

    _____

Living Out Our Transformation

Identify one way you can serve others with humility this week, trusting God to guide and strengthen you.

*   Building Deeper Connection to Transformation: Journaling Prompt: Reflect on times when you have led with humility. What did you learn from those experiences, and how can you apply those lessons now?

    _____

    _____

    _____

- Suggested Prayer: "Lord, help me to lead with humility and serve others with a heart that seeks to honor You. Guide me in my efforts and strengthen me in my journey. Amen."

_____

_____

_____

Tomorrow's Journey

Leading with humility opens the door for God to work through us. Tomorrow, we'll explore the importance of leading by example. Let's embrace humility in our leadership today.

DAY 5
LEADING BY EXAMPLE

Ever heard the saying, "Actions speak louder than words"? It's a classic adage that's been around longer than your grandma's secret recipe for meatloaf. Leading by example is all about walking the walk, not just talking the talk. It's about living in a way that inspires others to follow in your footsteps. Imagine a father teaching his child to ride a bike. The father doesn't just give instructions; he gets on his bike and shows his child how it's done, demonstrating patience, perseverance, and confidence. This hands-on approach is a perfect example of leading by example.

Today, we'll dive into the life of Timothy, the poster child for leading by example. If this principle were an Olympic sport, Timothy would be the gold medalist. His journey shows us the power of living out our faith in a way that others can see and be inspired by. So, grab a seat and get ready to see this powerful principle in action through his incredible journey.

Role Models in Scripture

Timothy, a young leader mentored by the Apostle Paul, exemplifies what it means to lead by example. Paul's letters to Timothy are filled with encouragement and guidance, emphasizing the importance of setting a good example for others. Paul wrote to Timothy, "Don't let anyone look down on you because you are young, but set an example for the believers in speech, in conduct, in love, in faith and in purity" (1 Timothy 4:12).

Timothy's leadership was characterized by his faithfulness and integrity. Despite his youth, he gained the respect and trust of the believers he led. Timothy was known for his sincere faith, which had been nurtured by his grandmother Lois and his mother Eunice. This strong spiritual foundation enabled Timothy to lead with confidence and authenticity.

Paul's mentorship played a significant role in Timothy's development as a leader. He encouraged Timothy to be bold and to use his gifts for the glory of God. Timothy's willingness to learn and grow under Paul's guidance exemplifies the importance of humility and teachability in leadership.

Timothy faced numerous challenges as a young leader, including opposition from false teachers and the need to address issues within the church. However, his steadfast faith and commitment to God's truth helped him navigate these difficulties. Timothy's example shows us that leadership is not about age or experience but about living a life that reflects Christ.

One of the most remarkable aspects of Timothy's leadership was his ability to inspire others through his conduct. He lived out his faith in a way that was visible and impactful. Timothy's example encourages us to lead by living lives of integrity, love, and faith, inspiring those around us to follow Christ.

Scripture to Remember

"Don't let anyone look down on you because you are young, but set an example for the believers in speech, in conduct, in love, in faith and in purity."
—1 Timothy 4:12

"For this reason I remind you to fan into flame the gift of God, which is in you through the laying on of my hands."
—2 Timothy 1:6

"Whatever you have learned or received or heard from me, or seen in me—put it into practice. And the God of peace will be with you."
—Philippians 4:9

Consider This

Reflect on Timothy's example of leadership and how he inspired others through his conduct. Consider how you can set a good example in your own life, regardless of your age or experience. Spend time journaling about the areas where you can improve your example and positively influence those around you.

Questions for Reflection

1. How can you set a good example in your life?

_____

_____

_____

2. In what areas can you improve your conduct to better reflect Christ?

_____

_____

_____

3. Who in your life has set a positive example for you to follow?

_____

_____

_____

Living Out Our Transformation

Identify one specific area where you can set a better example this week, and take steps to live it out.

_____

_____

_____

_____

_____

_____

Building Deeper Connection to Transformation

- Journaling Prompt: Reflect on someone who has set a good example for you. How did their actions inspire you, and how can you emulate their example?

- Suggested Prayer: "Lord, help me to set a good example in my speech, conduct, love, faith, and purity. Guide me to live a life that reflects Your love and truth. Amen."

Tomorrow's Journey

Leading by example is about Living Out Our Transformation authentically. As we conclude this week, let's commit to being the leaders and lights God has called us to be, shining brightly in all we do.

WEEK 3 REFLECTION

As we come to the end of Week 3, take some time to reflect on what you have learned and how it has impacted your journey of discovering your identity in Christ. Use this space to jot down your thoughts, insights, and any actions you plan to take moving forward.

Reflection Questions

1. What key insights did I gain about my identity in Christ this week?

_____

_____

_____

2. How has my understanding of being a leader and light in the world deepened?

_____

_____

_____

3. In what ways have I experienced God's presence and guidance during this week?

_____

_____

_____

4. What challenges did I face, and how did I overcome them?

_____

_____

_____

Personal Reflections

1. What specific steps can I take to continue embracing my identity in Christ?

_____

_____

_____

2. How can I incorporate the lessons learned into my daily life?

_____

_____

_____

3. Are there any areas where I still struggle with my identity? How can I address them?

_____

_____

_____

Action Plan

List three practical actions you will take in the coming week to nurture your identity in Christ.

1. _____

    _____

2. _____

    _____

3. _____

    _____

PRAYER

Spend a few moments in prayer, asking God to help you integrate what you've learned into your daily life and to continue guiding you on your journey of discovering your true identity.

"Heavenly Father, thank You for the insights and growth I've experienced this week. Help me to carry these lessons into the coming days and to live out my identity in Christ with confidence and trust in You. Amen."

Additional Notes

Use this space to write down any additional thoughts, prayers, or reflections you have as you conclude this week.

_____

_____

_____

_____

_____

_____

PREPARING
FOR THE FUTURE

As we conclude this devotional journey, take a moment to reflect on how far you have come and to prepare your heart and mind for continuing to grow in faith. Consider what you hope to achieve and how you will continue to seek God's guidance and strength.

Welcome to a lifetime of deepening faith and trust. May God bless you richly as you continue to strengthen your relationship with Him.

PRAYER FOR TRANSFORMATION:
Embracing Spiritual Growth

Opening:

> "Heavenly Father, I come before You with a humble heart, recognizing Your greatness and the depth of Your love for me."

Thanksgiving:

> "Thank You, Lord, for guiding me through this journey of embracing spiritual growth. I am grateful for the wisdom and insights You have provided along the way."

Reflection:

> "Lord, I have learned that true transformation is built on allowing Your Spirit to work within me, understanding Your Word, and cultivating a relationship with You through prayer and spiritual disciplines. I recognize the importance of daily

commitment to growing spiritually and becoming more like Christ."

Petitions:

"Father, I ask for Your strength and guidance as I continue to embrace spiritual growth. Help me to trust in Your process and rely on Your strength, especially in times of doubt and difficulty. Fill me with Your Spirit so that I may be transformed into Your likeness and live out Your will in my life."

Commitment:

"I commit to nurturing my spiritual growth each day, dedicating time to prayer, scripture reading, and reflection. Help me to stay rooted in Your Word and to live out my faith in every aspect of my life."

Intercession:

"I also lift up those who are struggling in their spiritual journey. May they find comfort and assurance in You. Use me, Lord, to support and encourage them as they seek to grow closer to You."

Closing:

"I ask all these things in the precious name of Jesus Christ, my Savior. Amen."

ADDITIONAL RESOURCES

Books and Articles

Books: Suggested readings for deeper understanding.

"The Purpose Driven Life" by Rick Warren

This bestselling book offers a 40day spiritual journey that will help you discover and live out God's purpose for your life. It provides practical insights and biblical principles to guide you in understanding your identity and calling.

"Celebration of Discipline" by Richard J. Foster

This classic work explores the spiritual disciplines that lead to deeper spiritual growth and transformation. Foster's book offers practical guidance on practices such as prayer, fasting, and meditation.

"The Practice of the Presence of God" by Brother Lawrence

A timeless Christian classic, this book teaches the importance of continually living in God's presence. Brother Lawrence's insights offer profound wisdom on how to integrate faith into everyday life.

"Spiritual Disciplines for the Christian Life" by Donald S. Whitney

Whitney provides a comprehensive guide to the spiritual disciplines essential for growth in godliness. This book is practical, biblical, and perfect for those seeking to deepen their spiritual lives.

"Forgotten God: Reversing Our Tragic Neglect of the Holy Spirit" by Francis Chan

In this book, Chan challenges believers to understand and embrace the Holy Spirit's power and presence in their lives, leading to true spiritual transformation.

Articles: Recommended articles for further insight.

"Spiritual Growth: The Journey of Becoming More Like Jesus" on Crosswalk

This article offers practical advice and biblical wisdom on the journey of spiritual growth, emphasizing the importance of daily commitment and the role of the Holy Spirit.

"The Transforming Power of the Holy Spirit" on Desiring God

Desiring God provides an insightful article that explores how the Holy Spirit works in our lives to bring about transformation, encouraging believers to rely on His power and guidance.

"Understanding the Spiritual Disciplines" on Bible Study Tools

This article explains the various spiritual disciplines and how they contribute to our spiritual growth. It offers practical steps for incorporating these practices into daily life.

"Living Out Your Spiritual Transformation" on Relevant
Magazine
Relevant Magazine discusses practical ways to live out spiritual
transformation daily, providing actionable advice and scriptural support
to help believers walk confidently in their faith.

Online Resources

Desiring God (www.desiringgod.org)
Desiring God offers a wealth of articles, sermons, and resources
focused on helping believers find joy and purpose in God. It's a
great site for deepening your understanding of spiritual growth and
transformation.

Crosswalk (www.crosswalk.com)
Crosswalk provides a variety of resources, including articles,
devotionals, and videos, to help Christians grow in their faith and
understand their spiritual journey.

Bible Study Tools (www.biblestudytools.com)
This site offers extensive resources for Bible study, including
articles, commentaries, and study guides that can aid in understanding
and embracing spiritual disciplines.

Relevant Magazine (www.relevantmagazine.com)
Relevant Magazine covers contemporary Christian issues and
provides articles that challenge and inspire believers to live out their
faith authentically.

These resources will support and enhance your journey of embracing spiritual growth and transformation. Whether through books, articles, or online resources, you'll find a wealth of knowledge and inspiration to help you grow in your faith and live out your Godgiven purpose.

ABOUT THE AUTHOR

Hey there! I'm Eric G Reid, Co-Founder and Editor-in-Chief at Skinny Brown Dog Media. My passion is helping folks like you discover and share your unique stories and identities. With over a decade of experience in digital media and publishing, I'm all about helping others find their true voice and purpose through the power of storytelling.

I got into publishing because I've always loved writing and wanted to help others tell their tales. As an author myself, I understand the thrill and challenge of bringing stories to life. Over the years, I've had the pleasure of working with a diverse bunch of authors, speakers, and coaches, each with their own unique voice. This journey has taught me just how transformative words can be and how important it is to be genuine in our storytelling.

When I'm not working with words, I love spending time with my family and my big yellow dog, Max. These moments recharge me and inspire my passion for helping others. If you want to connect, shoot me an email at Eric@SkinnyBrownDogMedia.com.

Looking forward to being a part of your journey of self-discovery and storytelling.

ABOUT THE A WHOLE LIFE DEVOTIONAL SERIES

Welcome to the Whole Life Devotional Series. Think of it as a spiritual road trip through different parts of your faith journey. Each book is like a friendly guide, helping you explore God's love, beef up your faith, and figure out how to live a life that really matters.

I am not about fancy theological jargon here. Instead, I am an authentic voice and practical insights, biblical wisdom, and real-life stories that'll help you grow closer to God. The series is intended to feel like you are a chat with a good friend who just happens to be pretty passionate about personal growth and faith stuff.

Feel free to drop me a line at Eric@SkinnyBrownDogMedia. com. I'd love to hear from you as we dive into this adventure of figuring out who God made us to be. Let's grow together!

Books in the Series:

Identity: Discovering Who You Are

- Focus: Understanding and embracing your identity in Christ.
- Themes: Self-worth, God's love, being made in God's image.
- Summary: Discover your true identity in Christ and replace the world's misconceptions with the solid truth of God's Word.

Faith: Strengthening Your Relationship with God

- Focus: Deepening your faith and spiritual growth.
- Themes: Prayer, Bible study, spiritual disciplines.
- Summary: Cultivate a vibrant, everyday faith that transforms your life in tangible ways.

Transformation: Embracing Spiritual Growth

- Focus: Becoming more Christlike through spiritual growth.
- Themes: Sanctification, growth in virtues, spiritual maturity.
- Summary: Embrace the process of spiritual transformation and grow deeper in your relationship with God.

Wisdom: Making Godly Decisions

- Focus: Making wise, biblically based decisions.
- Themes: Discernment, moral choices, God's guidance.
- Summary: Learn to make wise decisions that align with God's will and seek His divine guidance.

Surrender: Embracing God's Will

- Focus: Surrendering to God's will.
- Themes: Trust, obedience, letting go, faith.
- Summary: Understand and practice the concept of surrender, letting go of your own plans, and embracing God's perfect will.

Peace: Finding Rest in a Busy World

- Focus: Finding true rest and peace in God.
- Themes: Stress management, trust in God, spiritual rest.
- Summary: Find peace and rest through trust in God and learn practical steps to manage stress and embrace spiritual rest.

Additional books in the series are currently under consideration by the publisher. Please follow for updates and announcements on upcoming releases. Stay connected and be the first to know about new titles and insights designed to deepen your spiritual journey.

I AM
TRANSFORMED BY FAITH

A NEW CREATION IN CHRIST:

"Therefore, if anyone is in Christ, the new creation has come:
The old has gone, the new is here!"

—2 Corinthians 5:17

TRANSFORMED BY THE RENEWING OF YOUR MIND:

"Do not conform to the pattern of this world, but be transformed by the
renewing of your mind. Then you will be able to test and approve what
God's will is—his good, pleasing and perfect will."

—Romans 12:2

SANCTIFIED THROUGH FAITH:

"It is because of him that you are in Christ Jesus, who has become for us
wisdom from God—that is, our righteousness, holiness and redemption."

—1 Corinthians 1:30

EMPOWERED BY THE HOLY SPIRIT:

"But you will receive power when the Holy Spirit comes on you;
and you will be my witnesses in Jerusalem, and in all Judea and Samaria,
and to the ends of the earth."

—Acts 1:8

WALKING IN NEWNESS OF LIFE:

"We were therefore buried with him through baptism into death in order that, just as Christ was raised from the dead through the glory of the Father, we too may live a new life."

—Romans 6:4

BEARING THE FRUIT OF THE SPIRIT:

"But the fruit of the Spirit is love, joy, peace, forbearance, kindness, goodness, faithfulness, gentleness and self-control."

—Galatians 5:2223

LIVING OUT GOOD WORKS:

"For we are God's handiwork, created in Christ Jesus to do good works, which God prepared in advance for us to do."

—Ephesians 2:10

CONFORMED TO THE IMAGE OF CHRIST:

"For those God foreknew he also predestined to be conformed to the image of his Son, that he might be the firstborn among many brothers and sisters."

—Romans 8:29

STRENGTHENED IN YOUR INNER BEING:

"I pray that out of his glorious riches he may strengthen you with power through his Spirit in your inner being."

—Ephesians 3:16

GROWING IN GRACE AND KNOWLEDGE:

"But grow in the grace and knowledge of our Lord and Savior Jesus Christ. To him be glory both now and forever! Amen."

—2 Peter 3:18

ABIDING IN CHRIST:

"If you remain in me and I in you, you will bear much fruit;
apart from me you can do nothing."

JOHN 15:5

REFLECTING GOD'S GLORY:

"And we all, who with unveiled faces contemplate the Lord's glory,
are being transformed into his image with ever increasing glory,
which comes from the Lord, who is the Spirit."

—2 Corinthians 3:18

TRANSFORMED BY THE SPIRIT:

"But we all, with unveiled face, beholding as in a mirror the glory of the
Lord, are being transformed into the same image from glory to glory,
just as from the Lord, the Spirit."

—2 Corinthians 3:18

A LIVING SACRIFICE:

"Therefore, I urge you, brothers and sisters, in view of God's mercy,
to offer your bodies as a living sacrifice, holy and pleasing to God—this is
your true and proper worship."

—Romans 12:1

TRANSFORMED INTO HIS LIKENESS:

"And just as we have borne the image of the earthly man,
so shall we bear the image of the heavenly man."

—1 Corinthians 15:49